Mummies

Elizabeth Carney

NATIONAL GEOGRAPHIC
Washington, D.C.

For Patrick, Brendan, Brian, and Nora. Unlike mummies, laughing with you never gets old.—E.C.

Published by the National Geographic Society, Washington, D.C. 20036 All rights reserved.
Reproduction in whole or in part without written permission of the publisher is strictly prohibited.

Library of Congress Cataloging-in-Publication Data

Carney, Elizabeth, 1981-
Mummies / by Elizabeth Carney.
p. cm.
ISBN 978-1-4263-0528-3 (pbk. : alk. paper) -- ISBN 978-1-4263-0529-0 (library binding : alk. paper)
1. Mummies--Juvenile literature. I. Title.
GN293.C37 2009
393'.3--dc22
2009003630

Printed in the United States of America
09/WOR/1

Cover: © Todd Gipstein/ National Museum, Lima, Peru/ NationalGeographicStock.com; 1, 32 (middle, right): © DEA/ S. Vannini/ DeAgostini Picture Library/ Getty Images; 2: © ancientnile/ Alamy; 5 (both): © Christina Gascoigne/ Robert Harding Picture Library Ltd./ Alamy; 6: © Marwan Naamani/ AFP/ Getty Images; 7: © O. Louis Mazzatenta/ NationalGeographicStock.com; 8: © British Museum/ Art Resource, NY; 9, 32 (middle, left): © Glen Allison/ Photographer's Choice/ Getty Images; 10-11: © Robin Weaver/ Alamy; 12: © Vienna Report Agency/ Sygma/ Corbis; 13: © MARKA/ Alamy; 14-15: © Marc DeVille/ Getty Images; 16: © South American Pictures: 17: © Enrico Ferorelli; 18-19: © Illustration by Kimberly Schamber; 20: © Kenneth Garrett/ National Geographic/ Getty Images; 21: © AP Photo/ Ric Francis; 22: © Time Life Pictures/ Getty Images; 23 (top): © Robert Harding World Imagery/ Corbis; 23 (right): © Stapleton Collection/ Corbis; 24: © Erich Lessing/ British Museum/ Art Resource, NY; 25 (top): © Alistair Duncan/ Dorling Kindersley/ Getty Images; 25 (bottom): © Carl & Ann Purcell/ Corbis; 26, 27: © Hunan Provincial Museum; 29, 32 (bottom, left): © University College Museum, London, UK/ The Bridgeman Art Library; 30, 31: © Ira Block/ NationalGeographicStock.com; 32 (top, left): © Shutterstock; 32 (top, right): © Dr. Fred Hossler/ Visuals Unlimited/ Getty Images; 32 (bottom, right): © Bojan Brecelj/ Corbis

Table of Contents

Whoa, Mummy!

A farmer is working in
swampy land. His shovel hits
something hard. He uncovers
a blackened body.

It has hair, teeth, even fingerprints.
The farmer calls the police.
It looks like the person died recently.
But the body is over two thousand
years old! It's a mummy!

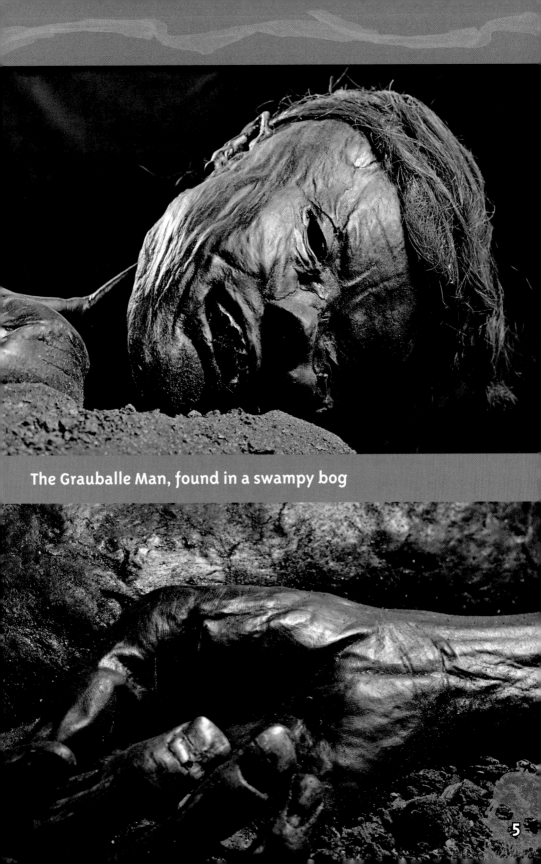

The Grauballe Man, found in a swampy bog

Mummy Making

When something dies, it decays. Insects, wild animals, and bacteria eat parts of the body.

A mummy is a dead body that doesn't decay.

A mummy can be made in two ways.

People can use bacteria-killing chemicals to make mummies.

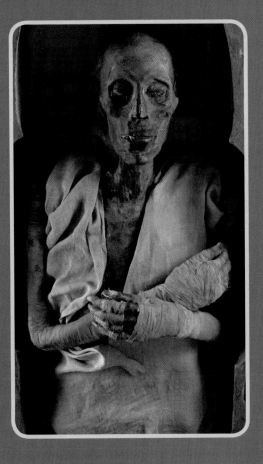

Or, if a body is in the right place at the right time, it can also become a mummy naturally. In those places, any dead body might become a mummy!

Word Wrap

BACTERIA: Tiny living things that can only be seen through a microscope.

DECAY: To rot or break down.

Natural Mummies

A bog mummy known as the Lindow Man

Body-eating bacteria do not grow well in places that are very cold. Or in places that are hot and dry. Or in places called bogs. People have found mummies on frosty mountaintops and in hot deserts.

Bogs are wet, swamp-like places. Bog mummies can be so well kept that scientists could tell one ancient man used hair gel!

Word Wrap

BOGS: Swampy areas where special mosses grow. The plants make the area a tough place for bacteria to live.

The man's face looks like he's sleeping. But he didn't die peacefully.

This bog mummy in Denmark was found with a rope around his neck. Experts think the man was killed as part of a religious ceremony.

The bits of his last meal, vegetable soup eaten 2,300 years ago, are still in his stomach.

Tollund Man

Ötzi Man

In 1991, two hikers found a man frozen in the mountains between Italy and Austria. A 5,300-year-old murder mystery! The mummy, nicknamed Ötzi (OOT-zee), is one of the oldest mummies ever found.

He wears a cape and leather shoes. But when scientists took a closer look at Ötzi's body, they found a surprise. A stone arrowhead was stuck in his shoulder. Ötzi had been shot in the back! Who killed Ötzi over five thousand years ago and why? So far the case has gone cold!

Ötzi as he might have looked

Man-made Mummies

For thousands of years, people have made mummies. Many cultures believed that a person's spirit lives on after death.

CULTURE: A group of people who share beliefs and customs

They thought spirits might need things in the next life. That's why mummies were sometimes buried with weapons, jewelry, food, or even mummies of favorite pets.

Different cultures had their own ways of making mummies. Some dried the bodies with sand or smoke. Others used chemicals to preserve bodies.

The first people to make mummies
may have been the Chinchorros.

Their mummies are 7,000 years old!
They are the oldest man-made
mummies ever found.

The Chinchorros mummified everyone who died, from babies to the oldest adults. They covered their mummies' faces with clay masks. Then the mummies were painted to make them black and shiny.

The culture disappeared around 3,000 years ago. These strange mummies were all that was left behind.

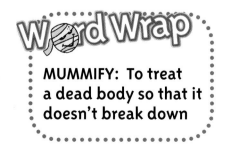

W✪rd Wrap

MUMMIFY: To treat a dead body so that it doesn't break down

How to Make a Mummy

1

2

3

LUNGS LIVERS

Workers remove organs such as the lungs and liver.

Mummy makers take out the brain through the nose with a large hook.

Workers wash the body and cover it with salts.

4

The body is
left to dry for
40 days.

5

Workers rub
scented oils on
the mummy.

6

Workers wrap the
mummy in linen.

Tomb of Treasures

Ancient Egyptians made millions of mummies. In 1922, a scientist named Howard Carter found a special mummy in Egypt. Carter peeked into a dark tomb and was struck with amazement. Gold sparkled everywhere.

Carter had found the tomb of Tutankhamun (toot-an-KAHM-uhn)! Known as King Tut, he died over 3,300 years ago. He was only 18 years old. But the young king was buried with priceless treasures. Tut's tomb made him the most famous mummy in the world.

TOMB: A grave, room, or building for holding a dead body

A Mummy's Curse

Howard Carter in the tomb
of King Tutankhamun

After the discovery of King Tut's tomb, people everywhere wanted to know more about the boy king. But not everything reported about Tut was true.

Shortly after the tomb was opened, one of Tut's discoverers died. Some people said that the boy king put a curse on the tomb.

Animal Wraps

Ancient Egyptians didn't just make human mummies. They made many animal mummies too!

Favorite pets were sometimes mummified and buried with their owners. Egyptians thought cats were very special. Sometimes, when a cat died, the whole family would mourn its death.

Egyptians also made mummies of dogs, crocodiles, monkeys, and birds. These animals were believed to please the gods.

MOURN: To feel or express sorrow or grief

Lovely Lady Mummy

Lady Dai may have looked like this.

Over 2,000 years ago, a wealthy Chinese woman known as Lady Dai died.

Her body was treated with salt. Salt takes water out of the body, which helps to keep it from rotting. The body was wrapped in 20 layers of silk.

Lady Dai was put into a nest of six beautifully painted coffins. Workers buried her at the bottom of a tunnel dug deep in the ground.

The tomb was shut tight with clay and mud. Workmen found Lady Dai in 1972. Her body was in such good shape that her skin and hair were still soft.

Mummies Today

Mummy-making is not just a thing of the ancient past. Some famous people have been mummified since then.

English thinker Jeremy Bentham died in 1832. He wanted his body to be used for science. Students took out his insides. They mummified his head. Then they dressed his skeleton in clothes. You can still go see him in England!

Secrets Unwrapped

Mummies can't talk. But they can still tell us many secrets about the past. Scientists study everything in and around a mummy's body.

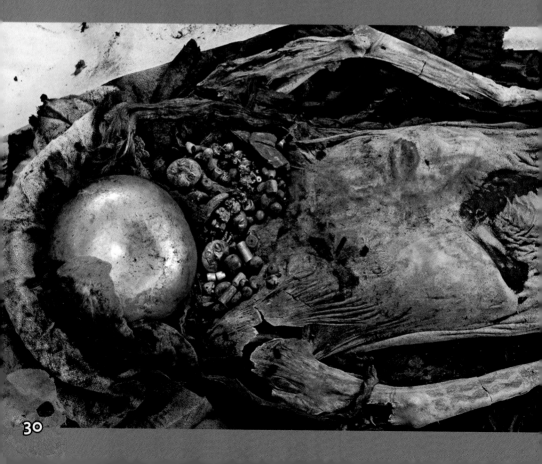

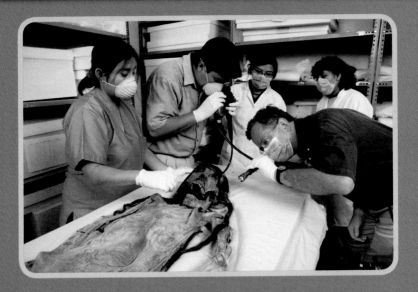

Food left in a mummy's stomach
tells about what people ate.
Broken bones tell about a person's life
and sometimes about his or her death.
Scientists can also examine a mummy's
clothes and the objects buried with it.

All hold clues to peoples'
religions and ways of life. In a way,
mummies are like time machines.

They give us a peek into the past.

DECAY
To rot or break down

BACTERIA
Tiny living things that can only be seen through a microscope. Bacteria can cause human diseases.

BOGS
Swampy areas where special mosses grow. The plants make the area a tough place for bacteria to live.

TOMB
A grave, room, or building for holding a dead body

MUMMIFY
To treat a dead body so that it doesn't break down

CULTURE
A group of people who share beliefs and customs

Dear Reader,

See if you can use all your new science words to finish this story!

I'm hunting mummies! I walk deeper into a dark _____.

Will I find a good mummy? It is not easy to _____

someone. And if you don't get it right, the body gets

eaten by_____and then it will _____.

Mummy hunters are always bummed out when this hap-

pens. When I need to beat the heat in Egypt, I'll head

north to Europe's swampy _____. Different place, different

_____, but it's all about the mummy to me.

NATIONAL GEOGRAPHIC KIDS™

National Geographic Readers

The easy-to-read books for curious kids!

LEVEL 2

For kids who are reading independently

ISBN 978-1-4263-0428-6   ISBN 978-1-4263-0426-2   ISBN 978-1-4263-0285-5   ISBN 978-1-4263-0286-2

There is a National Geographic Reader for every reading level.

Level 2 books are perfect for kids who are ready for longer sentences and more complex vocabulary. New words are defined on the page, but occasional adult help might be welcome.

U.S. $3.99 / $4.99 CAN

National Geographic's net proceeds support vital exploration, conservation, research, and education programs.

NATIONAL GEOGRAPHIC

ISBN 978-1-4263-0528-3 / PRINTED IN USA

50399

9 781426 305283

Contents

Gotham City

Gotham City is a busy place, with lots of citizens.

Commissioner Jim Gordon is the Head of Police. It is his job to stop crime in the city.

Jim is soon going to retire from the job. His daughter, Barbara, is going to take over.

The Hero Team

Sometimes, Gotham City
needs heroes! When a mission
is too dangerous for the police
alone, the police commissioner
shines the Bat-Signal.
Batman sees its light shining
and rushes to the rescue.
Batman likes to work alone,
but sometimes he needs help.
Robin and Batgirl help
him to catch criminals
and save the day.
Three heroes are
better than one!

COMMISSIONER JIM GORDON

— WANTS YOU TO HELP KEEP —

GOTHAM CITY SAFE

Citizens of Gotham City, please alert the police if you see any of the following:

 A **cat-like** woman prowling around jewelry stores.

 A man holding a giant **question mark**. Do not approach him! Conversation may cause confusion.

 A red-haired woman surrounded by wriggling **plants**.

 A man with a huge, **toothy grin**. Do not be fooled by his friendly appearance!

GOTHAM CITY POLICE DEPARTMENT

I BELIEVE IN BATMAN

Meet the Rogues

Gotham City's villains have started working together, too. Their team is known as the Rogues.

Each of these crooks has fought
Batman many times in the past.
He has beaten each one alone,
but never all of them at once!
Batman will have to use all of
his gadgets to save the day.

The Joker

The Joker is Batman's
foe. He likes to cause
trouble and create
chaos in the city.
The only thing that
the Joker takes seriously
is committing crime.

The Joker believes
he is Batman's worst
enemy. Batman does not
agree. This wipes the
smile off the Joker's face.

13

My <u>Worst</u> Enemy

by the Joker

Batman never laughs at my jokes, even though they are really funny!

He always tries to stop me from getting away from crime scenes.

He thinks he is really strong, but I always have the last laugh!

Batman likes to take pictures without me in them!

Harley Quinn

Harley Quinn is one of the Joker's closest allies. She loves his silly pranks and nasty tricks. Her colorful costume and bright makeup are nearly as eye-catching as the Joker's.

Harley used to be a doctor, but now she causes chaos. Batman should watch out for her swinging bat.

The Joker's Notorious Lowrider

The car can bounce up and down

Silly golden chicken decoration

Joker

Wheels spinning at top speed

The Joker and Harley Quinn drive around Gotham City in the Joker's Notorious Lowrider. They create as much chaos as they can. This wacky vehicle looks harmless, but it is perfect for scaring people!

Music system hides button for missile launcher

Handles for Harley Quinn to grip on to while skating

A missile launcher is hidden inside the trunk

Horn to make people jump

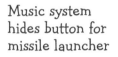

The Riddler

One of the most confusing criminals in Gotham City is the Riddler. He leaves tricky puzzles at crime scenes for Batman to solve.

If Batman follows the tire tracks of the Riddler's Riddle Racer, he might be able to stop this Rogue once and for all. Or could this be another trick?

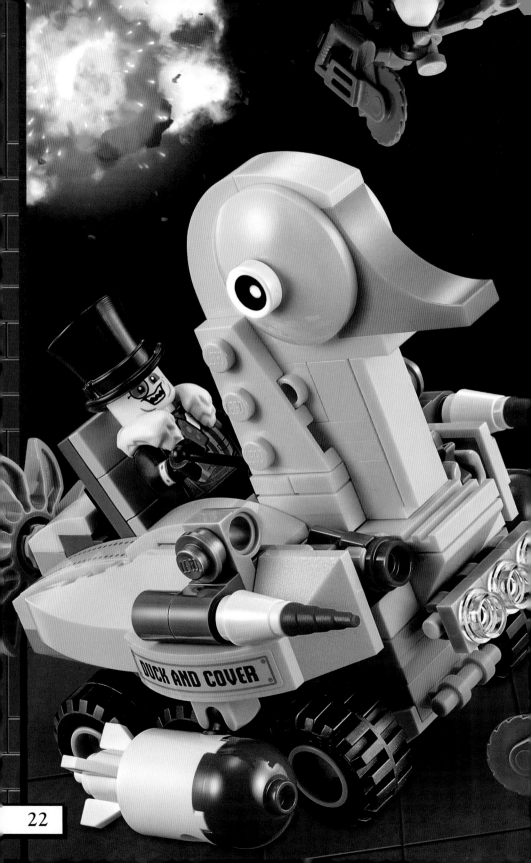

DUCK AND COVER

The Penguin

This businessman is no birdbrain!
The Penguin controls lots of gangs
in Gotham City. This has made
him very rich. He wears an
expensive top hat and suit.

The Penguin attacks Batman's
Batcave with an army of penguin
friends. His getaway vehicle is
shaped like a duck.

Mr. Freeze

This frosty villain sends a chill
down Batman's spine. He wears
a large, armored suit that keeps
him ice-cold at all times.

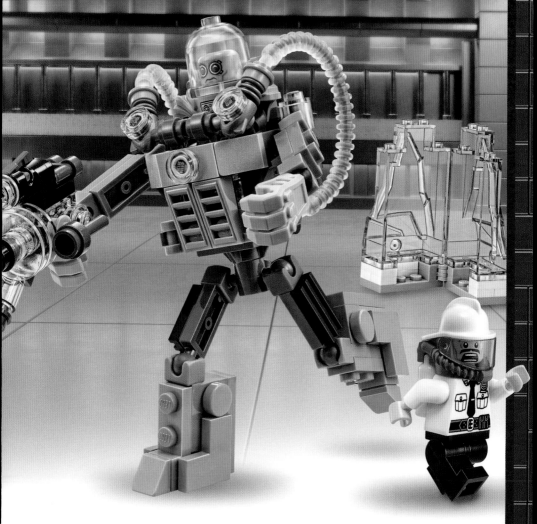

Mr. Freeze is a scientist. He even
invented his own freeze gun.
He attacks the Gotham City
Energy Facility with the rest of the
Rogues. When he tells the scared
workers to "freeze," they really do!

Killer Croc

Killer Croc is one of Batman's most fearsome foes. He has a powerful tail, scaly skin, and snapping teeth—just like a real crocodile!

Catwoman makes a speedy getaway on her purple motorcycle. Luckily, Robin and Batgirl are right on her tail!

Poison Ivy

This Rogue likes plants much more than humans. Even her outfit is inspired by flowers. She has green-fingered gloves, and she wears leaves in her red hair.

Poison Ivy has special powers. She can control all forms of plant life. Poison Ivy wants to trap Batman in her tangling tendrils.

Clayface

Clayface is the biggest
and messiest of Batman's
foes. He is made of mud
and can transform into
different shapes. He
creates giant mud fists for
attacking his enemies.

Clayface loves to
destroy everything around
him. Batman must watch
out for the splats of mud
he fires to stick people to
the ground.

The Joker's Plan

The Joker is very smart. He has
come up with a cunning plan.
He wants to destroy Gotham City
Energy Facility, which supplies
all the power to the city. Gotham
City will be in total chaos and
the Joker will take over!

THE JOKER'S FUNHOUSE

Hi, everyone. It's the Joker! I have created my very own funhouse in Gotham City. Come inside. You won't be able to stop smiling. But you MUST follow these rules...

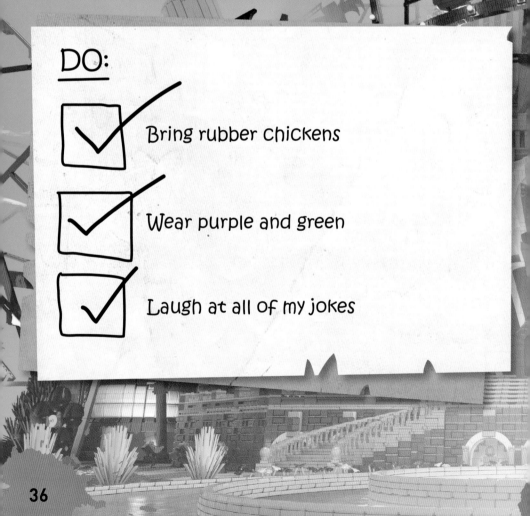

DO:

☑ Bring rubber chickens

☑ Wear purple and green

☑ Laugh at all of my jokes

DO NOT:

 Wear black (or yellow)

 Wear long black capes and drive bat-like vehicles

Wear black cowls with pointy ears

Gotham City's Villains

The Rogues aren't the only villains
in Gotham City. There are many
odd outlaws committing crimes.
There are villains dressed
as animals, like Zebra-Man,
March Harriet, and Orca.

The Mime

March Harriet

Orca

T. ERASE!

There are even villains who base their crimes on numbers, like The Calculator. All of these villains have one thing in common—they want to help the Joker defeat Batman!

Kite Man

The Eraser

Calendar Man

The Calculator

Zebra-Man

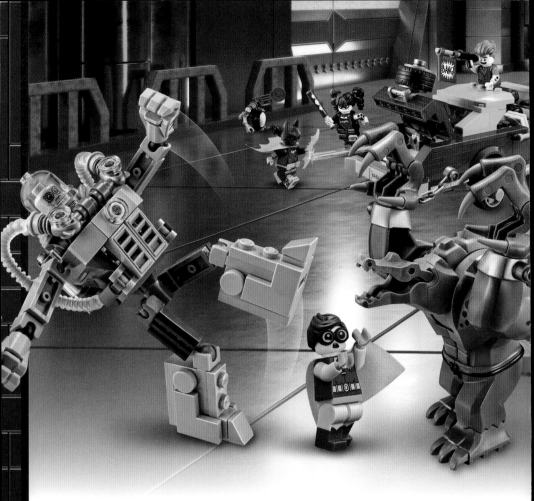

Villains vs. the Hero Team

The Joker and his allies attack the Gotham City Energy Facility! It will take great teamwork for the Hero Team to defeat the villains.

Batman takes on Clayface and the Riddler. Robin tackles Mr. Freeze and Killer Croc. Batgirl battles with the Joker and Harley Quinn. The Hero Team must win!

Locked Up

Hurrah! Batman, Batgirl, and Robin have put an end to the Joker's plan and defeated him.

All of the Rogues have been captured. They are now locked up in Arkham Asylum. Gotham City is safe once more. Thanks, Hero Team!

Quiz

1. Who is going to take over from Jim Gordon as Head of Police?

2. What kind of hat does the Penguin wear?

3. How does the police commissioner ask Batman for help?

4. How does Poison Ivy plan to trap Batman?

5. What kind of weapon does Harley Quinn use?

6. What is Catwoman's favourite thing to steal?

7. What does the Joker want to destroy?

8. Where are the Rogues now locked up?

Answers on page 48

Glossary

allies
A group of people who work together for a purpose.

Arkham Asylum
A hospital where Gotham's worst criminals are locked away.

citizen
Someone who lives in a town or city.

crook
A person who is dishonest or a criminal.

fearsome
Very frightening.

foe
An enemy or opponent.

gang
An organised group of criminals.

scientist
A person who studies science and solves problems by doing experiments.

Guide for Parents

This book is part of an exciting four-level reading series for children, developing the habit of reading widely for both pleasure and information. These chapter books have a compelling main narrative to suit your child's reading ability. Each book is designed to develop your child's reading skills, fluency, grammar awareness, and comprehension in order to build confidence and engagement when reading.

Ready for a *Level 2* book

YOUR CHILD SHOULD

- be familiar with using beginning letter sounds and context clues to figure out unfamiliar words.
- be aware of the need for a slight pause at commas and a longer one at periods.
- alter his/her expression for questions and exclamations.

A VALUABLE AND SHARED READING EXPERIENCE

For many children, reading requires much effort, but adult participation can make this both fun and easier. So here are a few tips on how to use this book with your child.

TIP 1 Check out the contents together before your child begins:

- read the text about the book on the back cover.
- flip through the book and stop to chat about the contents page together to heighten your child's interest and expectation.
- make use of unfamiliar or difficult words on the page in a brief discussion.
- chat about the nonfiction reading features used in the book, such as headings, captions, lists, or charts.